Windsor Castle

OFFICIAL SOUVENIR GUIDE

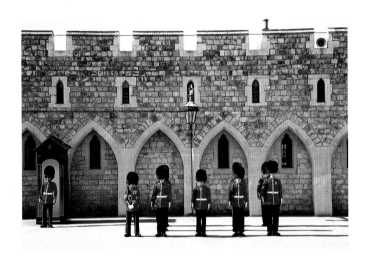

DIEU ET MON DROIT

Contents

Introduction

It is the most Romantique castle that is in the world.

Samuel Pepys, *Diary*, 1666

Windsor Castle was founded by William the Conqueror (r.1066–87) at the end of the eleventh century. It has been the home of 39 monarchs and is the oldest royal residence in the British Isles to have remained in continuous use.

The Castle is one of the official residences of Her Majesty Queen Elizabeth II. The Queen is Head of State of the United Kingdom of Great Britain and Northern Ireland, and Head of the Commonwealth.

The Queen is officially in residence at Windsor twice a year: at Easter, and again in June, when the annual Garter Service is held in St George's Chapel. The Castle is used as an alternative to Buckingham Palace for ceremonial visits by foreign heads of state. The Queen and The Duke of Edinburgh (b.1921) spend most of their private weekends at Windsor.

The State Apartments are frequently used by members of the Royal Family for events in support of organisations of which they are patrons, and for the annual Windsor Festival. Royal weddings, baptisms and birthday celebrations have been held at Windsor for centuries. These have included the marriage of The Prince of Wales (b.1948) and The Duchess of Cornwall (b.1947) at Windsor Guildhall in 2005.

The Castle is divided into three principal areas, known as wards. The steeply sloping Lower Ward is the most public part of the precincts. The Middle Ward is ranged around the Norman motte (mound), crowned by the Round Tower, which today accommodates the Royal Archives and the historic photographs in the Royal Collection. The Upper Ward, reached via the Norman Gate, contains the State Apartments and royal apartments, arranged around the great open space of the Quadrangle, which is sometimes used as a parade ground.

This official souvenir guide provides an account of the history of the Castle, as well as a guide to the State Apartments and to the magnificent works of art on display. Further sources of information are listed on the inside of the back cover flap.

OPPOSITE
Aerial view of the Upper and Middle Wards from the north-west.

LEFT
The Prince of Wales and The Duchess of Cornwall leaving St George's Chapel on their wedding day, 9 April 2005.

👑 Windsor Castle occupies 10.5 hectares.

👑 In the Upper Ward there are 951 rooms (including corridors and staircases), of which 225 are bedrooms.

👑 State Banquets are held in St George's Hall (55.5 x 9 metres), at a table seating up to 160 guests.

👑 The State Apartments have been open to the public throughout the year since the 1840s. During the winter period, from October to March, the tour is now extended to include the Semi-State Apartments (described on pp. 56–65). Use of the Castle by the Royal Family may sometimes cause the published opening times to vary for short periods.

BELOW
The official entrance to the State Apartments.

THE ROYAL COLLECTION

The Royal Collection is held by The Queen as Sovereign for her successors and the nation. Displayed within the State Apartments are some of the finest works of art in the Royal Collection, many of them still in the historic settings for which they were collected or commissioned by successive monarchs, notably George IV (r.1820–30). The revenue from admissions to Windsor Castle passes to the Royal Collection Trust, a registered charity that exists to preserve the collection and to make it as accessible as possible. A proportion of the income from visitors to the Castle is used to maintain the fabric of the Castle, and to run the College of St George.

LEFT
B.L. Vulliamy (1780–1854), gilt and patinated bronze clock, 1819.

More than 160 people live within the precincts of the Castle, including the Constable and Governor, the Dean of Windsor and Canons of the College of St George, and the Military Knights.

Over 200 people work at the Castle, among them maintenance staff, housekeepers, porters, a clockmaker, grooms and coachmen, furniture restorers, choristers, priests, police and soldiers, a flagman, the wardens and other staff who present the Castle to the public, librarians, curators, bookbinders, conservators and archivists. These numbers increase at Easter and in June, when the Court relocates to Windsor.

THE GUARDS AT WINDSOR

The soldiers on sentry duty within the precincts are usually drawn from the five regiments of Foot Guards (Coldstream, Grenadier, and Scots, Irish and Welsh Guards), of which one battalion is always stationed at Windsor. The Changing of the Guard routinely takes place at 11am on the parade ground in the Lower Ward. When the Court is in residence, the ceremony takes place in the Quadrangle.

ABOVE
Cleaning the 500-square-metre carpet in St George's Hall.

LEFT
Preparing the table in St George's Hall for a State Banquet.

History of the Castle

RIGHT & BELOW
Wenceslaus Hollar
(1607–77), *Perspective*
(detail) *and bird's eye view
of Windsor Castle*, 1672.
Etching.

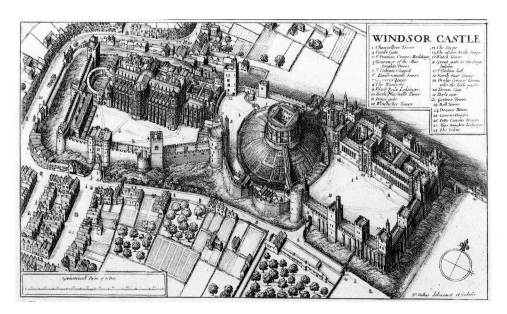

OPPOSITE
The door at the east end
of St George's Chapel
survives from Henry III's
original chapel. The
ironwork is signed by the
medieval smith,
Gilebertus, and gives an
idea of the high artistic
quality of Henry III's work
at Windsor.

Windsor Castle as it appears today is the result of almost a thousand years of development, but four monarchs in particular have left their mark: William the Conqueror, who founded the Castle and established its outline plan and extent; Edward III (r.1327–77), who rebuilt it in a magnificent Gothic style and established the royal apartments in the Upper Ward; Charles II (r.1660–85), who transformed the Upper Ward of the medieval castle into a baroque palace; and George IV, who restored the exterior to conform with romantic ideals of castle architecture, and created sumptuous and richly furnished palace interiors within the ancient fabric.

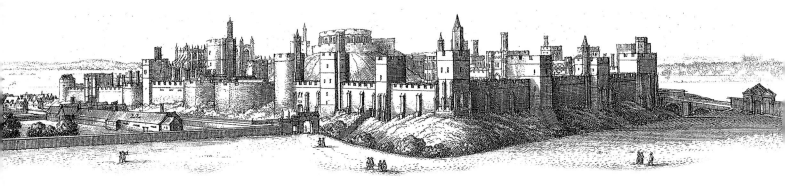

HISTORY OF THE CASTLE

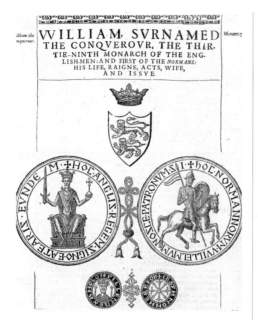

access from the capital and proximity to a
royal hunting forest (of which Windsor
Great Park is the surviving portion)
recommended it as a royal residence.
Henry I (r.1100–35) had domestic quarters
within the Castle as early as 1110, and his
grandson, Henry II (r.1154–89), built two
sets of apartments: a state residence in the
Lower Ward and a smaller family lodging
in the Upper Ward.

When first built, the Castle was walled in
timber. In the late twelfth century, Henry II
began to replace the outer fortifications in
stone; the original Norman keep was rebuilt
as the Round Tower in 1170. The outer walls
were punctuated with towers: those from
the reign of Henry II (as on the east front)
are generally square, whereas those from
the reign of his grandson, Henry III (r.1216–72),
are D-shaped. There is a well-preserved
section of Henry III's perimeter wall, with
its towers, not far from the Henry VIII Gate.

Willliam the Conqueror began building
at Windsor around 1070, and his
work was finished by 1086. The Castle was
built as one of a chain of fortifications
around London, and occupies the only
naturally defensive site in this part of the
Thames valley, 30 metres above the river.
Of the original group of castles, only
Windsor has survived intact. Norman castles
were built to a standard plan, with an
artificial earth mound supporting a keep
(motte), whose entrance was protected by a
fenced yard (bailey). At Windsor, unusually,
there were two baileys, known today as the
Upper and Lower Wards, either side of the
motte. The outer walls of the Castle were
surrounded by a ditch, only part of which
survives.

The Castle was built to secure the
western approach to London, but easy

MEDIEVAL EXPANSION

Edward III (r.1327–77), the 'warrior' King, best known for his lengthy campaigns in France during the Hundred Years War, spent £50,000 transforming Windsor from a military fortification to a Gothic palace. The massive architecture of Windsor reflects Edward III's ideal of a Christian, chivalric monarchy.

Work began with the Lower Ward, which was transformed by new buildings for the College of St George, founded in 1348. The chapel built there 100 years earlier by Henry III had been dedicated to St Edward the Confessor, but it was Edward III who first associated the Castle and the College with St George, the patron saint of the new Order of the Garter.

Reconstruction of the Upper Ward began in 1357, under the direction of William of

GALLETTING

Medieval masons used small chips of flint to act as spacers, ensuring that as each massive stone was lowered onto its bed of mortar, it formed part of a level course. Over the centuries, this technique, known as galletting, acquired an ornamental aspect. This purely decorative form can be found throughout the Castle's external masonry, but dates mainly from the early nineteenth century.

Wykeham, Bishop of Winchester (1324–1404). An inner gatehouse with cylindrical towers (misleadingly known as the Norman Gate) was built. On the north side of the Quadrangle, royal apartments, with separate rooms for the King and his Queen, Philippa of Hainault (c.1312–69), were arranged around a series of internal courts. The apartments were all on the first floor, supported by stone-vaulted undercrofts that accommodated the domestic offices. These vaulted spaces survive today.

William of Wykeham's new buildings for Edward III took the architecture of the Castle to a new level, beyond what was

This yeare [1359] the Kyng sette workemenne in hande to take downe muche olde buildings belonging to the Castel of Windsor, and caused divers other faire and sumptuous workes to bee erected and sette up in and aboute the same Castel, so that almoste all the masons and carpenters that were of any accounte within this lande were sente for …

Holinshed, *Chronicles*, 1577

necessary for purely defensive purposes. For example, the great range overlooking the Quadrangle and accommodating the King's Great Chambers, St George's Hall and the Royal Chapel was lit by 17 tall, arched windows, with two matching fortified entrance towers. Safely within the precincts of the Castle such defensive detailing was unnecessary, but this façade, 118 metres in length, was also intended to form a suitable backdrop for the magnificent tournaments staged within the Quadrangle, which acted as the Castle's tilt-yard. Tournaments were one aspect of the regular gatherings of Edward III's court at Windsor. Wardrobe accounts testify to the creation of the most elaborate costumes and crests, including one worn by the King in 1339 containing 3,000 peacock feathers. The helms and banners of today's Knights of the Garter, in the Quire (choir) of St George's Chapel, descend from these origins.

The fourteenth-century apartments essentially survived until the seventeenth century. Edward III's great-grandson, Edward IV (r.1461–83), began the present St George's Chapel to the west of Henry III's chapel. The latter, now known as the Albert Memorial Chapel, was substantially rebuilt by Henry VII (r.1485–1509), the first Tudor monarch, who also extended to the west of the State Apartments in 1500, probably to accommodate his own private study and library.

ABOVE
The Great Kitchen, with its fourteenth-century timber skylight, is the oldest working kitchen in England.

THE GOTHIC STYLE AT WINDSOR
The Gothic style of building, with pointed arches and fan vaulting, as seen in both St George's Chapel and (here) in the Grand Vestibule (*c*.1800–04), has remained the predominant architectural style at Windsor for 800 years.

ABOVE
James Stephanoff (1789–1874), *The Great Kitchen*, 1817. Watercolour.

TUDOR WINDSOR

At the time of his death in January 1547, Henry VIII (r.1509–47) owned 60 houses and palaces. The King travelled with his household between his many residences, which were furnished and made ready in advance of his arrival, but stood empty for the rest of the year. It was at Windsor, in 1522, that he received the Holy Roman Emperor Charles V, in order to conclude an alliance against France. Henry VIII's most significant additions to the fabric of Windsor were the gate that bears his name at the bottom of the Lower Ward, through which visitors leave the precincts, and the terrace (wharf) along the north side of the external walls of the Upper Ward, constructed in 1533–4. This was built of timber and supported an arbour, from which the King could watch the hunt in the park below. Henry also used the terrace to practise shooting at targets, while elsewhere he refurbished his father's 'tennis-play' (tennis court) at the foot of the motte adjacent to Engine Court.

Henry VIII was buried in St George's Chapel, alongside his third and favourite wife, Jane Seymour (c.1509–37), who had died shortly after giving birth to the future Edward VI (r.1547–53). A grandiose monument to King Henry was intended to have been set up in Henry VII's chapel, incorporating a sarcophagus originally intended for Cardinal Wolsey (c.1475–1530); although certain parts of the monument were cast in bronze, it remained unfinished, and all trace of it was removed during the Civil War.

In 1549, the new King, Edward VI, complained of Windsor: 'Methinks I am in a prison; here be no galleries, nor no gardens to walk in'; but his life and reign were too short to allow any improvements to the Castle. His half-sister, Mary I (r.1553–8), refaced many of the houses for the Military Knights in the Lower Ward, and her arms – together with those of her Spanish husband, Philip II (1527–98) – can be found on the old belfry tower, known today as Mary Tudor Tower, the residence of the Governor of the Military Knights.

By the reign of Elizabeth I (r.1558–1603), many parts of the Castle were in need of repair, and an extensive campaign of work was undertaken in the 1570s. Henry VIII's terrace walk was described as 'in verie great ruyn'. Likewise the medieval Royal Chapel, at the western end of St George's Hall, overlooking the Quadrangle, was 'very ould ruinous and far oute of order redie to fale downe'.

The terrace walk was entirely renewed in stone, with an elaborately ornamented balustrade, while the Royal Chapel was remodelled and refitted with stalls, a gallery and a panelled ceiling.

Overlooking the North Terrace, adjacent to the privy lodgings added by her grandfather Henry VII, Queen Elizabeth built a long gallery intended as a place to walk and admire the far prospects to the north during inclement weather. The Queen 'took great Delight in being out in the Air', but hated 'to be russled by the wind'. Her gallery was transformed as part of the Royal Library during the nineteenth century.

RIGHT
Marcus Gheeraerts I (1516/21–c.1590), *Procession of the Knights of the Garter, with the Sword-Bearer and Queen Elizabeth, with a view of Windsor Castle in the background*, 1576. Etching with hand-colouring. The new North Terrace Walk can be seen below the north front of the Castle.

W hen conflict broke out between Crown and Parliament in 1642, many of the royal palaces were commandeered by the Parliamentarian forces, often resulting in destruction or sale, but the troops were ordered to 'take some especial care' of Windsor. Despite this, the treasury of St George's Chapel was ransacked and some of its monuments desecrated. The King's nephew, Prince Rupert of the Rhine (1619–82), led an unsuccessful attempt to recapture the Castle, which was frequently used by Oliver Cromwell as his headquarters, and as a prison for captured Royalist officers. When the King himself returned, it was as

a prisoner, for his last Christmas. After his execution on 30 January 1649, his body was brought to St George's Chapel and buried in the vault occupied by the remains of Henry VIII.

Following the Restoration of the monarchy in 1660, the former life of the Castle was slowly resumed. The buildings of St George's were reoccupied by the clergy, and the houses in the Lower Ward were rid of squatters. In 1668, Prince Rupert was appointed Constable of the Castle, and instituted a new programme of repairs and redecoration.

ABOVE
C.W. Cope (1811–90), *The burial of Charles I at Windsor*, 1861 (detail). Mural decoration for the Peers' Corridor of the Palace of Westminster.

LEFT
School of Sir Peter Lely (1618–80), *Prince Rupert of the Rhine*, c.1666–80.

Prince Rupert … handsomely adorned his hall with furniture of arms, which was very singular, by so disposing the pikes, muskets, pistols, bandoleers, holsters, drums, back, breast, and head-pieces … as to represent festoons, and that without any confusion, trophy-like.

John Evelyn, *Diary*, 1670

ARMS AND ARMOUR

BELOW

Diego de Çaias
(*fl. c.*1535–52), Henry VIII's
hunting sword and knife,
1544 (in the Queen's Guard
Chamber). This sword was
intended to be used in
hunting; the scabbard comes
with the smaller knife for
dealing with dead quarry.
The sword blade is decorated
with a military scene
celebrating Henry VIII's
successful siege of Boulogne
in 1544.

BELOW

Diamond-hilted sword, *c.*1750
and *c.*1820 (in the Queen's
Guard Chamber). This sword
was purchased by George IV in
1820, who had the royal
goldsmiths, Rundell, Bridge &
Rundell, add several hundred
further stones, including the
two large diamonds on the
scabbard. The steel blade was
made at the same time and
decorated with the national
flowers of Great Britain and
other royal devices.

ABOVE

Henry VIII's armour. This magnificent suit of armour
was made at Greenwich around 1540 and is now
displayed in the Lantern Lobby. Several 'exchange'
pieces, to adapt the armour for the different exercises
of the tournament, are shown in the Queen's Guard
Chamber. The armour records the King's impressive
physical proportions, which were quite exceptional in
the sixteenth century.

CHARLES II AND THE 'ENGLISH VERSAILLES'

RIGHT
Antonio Verrio, *Charles II*,
c.1683 (fragment of the
painted plaster ceiling of
St George's Hall).

Charles II (r.1660–85) was determined to reinstate Windsor Castle as his principal non-metropolitan palace. It was his father's burial-place, and his restoration of the Castle, and of the full ceremonial of the Garter, were important symbols of the Restoration of the monarchy itself. The gentleman-architect Hugh May (1621–84) had been in exile with the King in Holland; in 1673 he was appointed to supervise the modernisation of the royal apartments, which were to become the grandest baroque State Apartments in England. The work took 11 years to complete.

Hugh May's work entailed extensive refenestration. The ancient defensive walls were now pierced by tall, round-headed windows; and on the north side, the ancient line of the Castle wall was broken through to form the principal royal lodgings. The new apartments created for the King and his Queen, Catherine of Braganza (1638–1705), followed the sequence that had evolved over several hundred years. They occupied much the same spaces as former monarchs had used, but the architecture and decoration were now dictated by the strict protocol of the restored court. Each set of apartments began with a guard chamber bristling with weaponry, reminding the visitor that the royal persons were well guarded. There followed, in succession, the presence chamber, privy chamber, withdrawing room, great and little bedchambers, and closet.

Charles II specified that 'all persons or gentlemen of quality and good fortune' and 'all wives and daughters of the nobility' should be allowed to pass into the Presence Chamber. The King conducted most of his important business in the withdrawing room, great chamber and private rooms beyond, to which access was strictly regulated.

May assembled a formidable team of artists and craftsmen to work throughout the new apartments. The Neapolitan mural painter, Antonio Verrio (c.1640–1721), was appointed 'Servant in Ordinary to his Majesty imployed in Paynting and adorning

BELOW
Sir Peter Lely, *Self-portrait
with Hugh May*, c.1675.
The architect holds a plan
of the Castle, which also
appears in the
background.

His Majesty's building in Windsor Castle'. He painted 23 ceilings, and the walls of the staircases to the King's and Queen's apartments, with mythological scenes glorifying the restored dynasty; while in St George's Hall, the whole north wall (33.5 metres) was devoted to a victory procession for the Black Prince, greeted by his father, Edward III. The new St George's Hall was paved in black and white marble, and at its eastern end a broad, stepped dais supported an elaborately carved and gilded throne of state, surrounded by figures of Fame, Justice and Prudence.

These murals were accompanied by virtuoso compositions in carved limewood by Grinling Gibbons (1648–1721) and his assistant, Henry Phillips (*fl.* 1662–93). The richness of the apartments was everywhere heightened by expensive textiles: fringed velvets with gold and silver embroidery for the throne canopies and beds, and magnificent tapestries. The rooms were filled with works of art formerly in the collection of Charles I, sold under Cromwell, but subsequently recovered, such as the colossal portraits of the late King and his family by Van Dyck (1599–1641).

Charles II loved Windsor, particularly in late summer and autumn, when there would be hunting, and horseracing at Datchet. In 1674, he staged a re-creation of the siege of Maastricht (which had taken place the previous year) on the meadows between the Castle and the river, watched from the North Terrace by an audience of a thousand.

In his transformation of Windsor, completed in 1684, the King was conscious of the example of his first cousin, Louis XIV of France (1638–1715), who was undertaking an unprecedented campaign of building and artistic patronage, above all at Versailles and the Louvre, using architectural magnificence both as an instrument of diplomacy and as a demonstration of the permanence of his right to rule. The Long Walk, an avenue of elm trees stretching 4 kilometres to the south of the Castle, was planted from 1680 in much the same spirit. Charles II emulated his French cousin in other ways: there was a playhouse within the Castle, with a troupe of 'French comoedians'; and music was provided by a new court orchestra, known as the Twenty-Four Violins, based directly on that of Louis XIV.

Charles II's apartments survived virtually unchanged to the end of the eighteenth century. Among his immediate successors, William III (r.1689–1702) concentrated his attentions on the Tudor palace of Hampton Court, which was vastly extended by Sir Christopher Wren (1632–1723), and on Kensington Palace.

Queen Anne (r.1702–14), the daughter of James II (r.1685–8), was born at Windsor and retained a special affection for the Castle. She purchased and enlarged a small house, later known as the Queen's Garden House, on the south side. On coming to the throne, she took to using the modern State Apartments of her uncle, Charles II, but the Garden House remained her favourite Windsor residence.

GEORGE III: THE RETURN TO WINDSOR

ABOVE
Paul Sandby, *View of the Quadrangle*, 1770s. Watercolour.

RIGHT
After George Robertson (1748–88), *South-east view of Windsor Castle*, 1783. Engraving. The Queen's Lodge is the long building in the centre.

It was not until the reign of George III (r.1760–1820) that Windsor became an important centre of court life once again. For the first 20 years of his reign, George III made few changes, except for a vast extension to Queen Anne's Garden House, which took on a somewhat barrack-like appearance and became known as the Queen's Lodge. Partly designed by the King himself and partly by his architect William Chambers (1723–96), it was the Windsor residence of the King and Queen and their growing family.

George III was the first Hanoverian born and educated in Britain, and in his study of English history he absorbed the values of chivalry promoted at the time by scholars such as Richard Hurd, Bishop of Worcester (1720–1808), who was subsequently appointed tutor to George III's sons. Hurd probably inspired the King, in the 1780s,

to commission for Windsor from Benjamin West (1738–1820) an ambitious cycle of large-scale paintings of the life of Edward III and the Black Prince, in succession to those painted by Verrio for Charles II.

From 1781, when a set of apartments within the east range of the Upper Ward was refurbished for the use of George, Prince of Wales, the royal family gradually began to reoccupy the Castle. New rooms in the same area were provided for Queen Charlotte (1744–1818) in the 1790s, and several of the baroque State Apartments on the north side of the Quadrangle were given a neoclassical dressing. An emphatic change of tempo and style followed the appointment of James Wyatt (1746–1813) as Surveyor General of the Office of Works in 1796. Wyatt's facility in the Gothic style enabled George III, from 1800, to embark on a restoration of the external façades and the creation of a new Grand Staircase to the State Apartments, the plaster ceiling and lantern of which survive in the Grand Vestibule today. Once again at a time of national crisis, with the menace of republican France, Windsor was recognised as a symbolic bastion of monarchy and the nation. The re-gothicisation of the Castle, and renewed emphasis on chivalry and the Order of the Garter, may be seen as the King's response to the new threat.

Wyatt was also employed to extend and refurbish Frogmore House (see page 25), south of the Castle, as a retreat for Queen Charlotte. Here she built up a substantial library and collection of decorative art, assisted by her daughters.

WINDSOR UNIFORM

George III devised a special Windsor uniform, comprising full dress and undress coats, in navy blue with red facings. The uniform is worn at Windsor by members of the Royal Family today, and is reflected in the uniform worn by the wardens on duty when the Castle is open.

ABOVE
After James Pollard (1792–1859), *His Majesty King George III returning from hunting*, 1820. Hand-coloured aquatint. The King and his sons are wearing the Windsor uniform.

RIGHT
Windsor Castle Wardens.

BELOW
Paul Sandby, *View of the inside of the Henry VIII Gate*, 1770s. Watercolour.

GEORGE IV: A PALACE WITHIN A CASTLE

When George IV succeeded to the throne in 1820, he determined to continue the Gothic transformation of the Castle, combined with the creation of comfortable and palatial royal apartments. He was strongly influenced by his artistic adviser, Sir Charles Long (1760–1838). In 1823, Long drew up an informal brief for a competition for the work. George IV and Long intended that the exterior of Windsor should once more be given an imposing, castle-like appearance. This would entail the heightening of Henry II's Round Tower, the reclothing of the exterior in massive masonry, and the addition of towers and battlements. In the Upper Ward, long-standing problems of circulation between sets of private apartments on the south and east sides would be overcome by adding a gallery of 168 metres, the Grand Corridor, built in the Perpendicular Gothic style against the existing walls on the Quadrangle side. The State Apartments on the north side would be given a new grand entrance and staircase, with two colossal new spaces: the Waterloo Chamber, celebrating the defeat of Napoleon Bonaparte in 1815, and an extended St George's Hall, taking in the space once occupied by the Royal Chapel.

Leading architects were asked to submit plans, and the late James Wyatt's nephew, Jeffry Wyatt (1766–1840), was awarded the task. He carried out Long's programme to the last detail, creating the present appearance of the Upper Ward. He earned a knighthood and the King's permission to

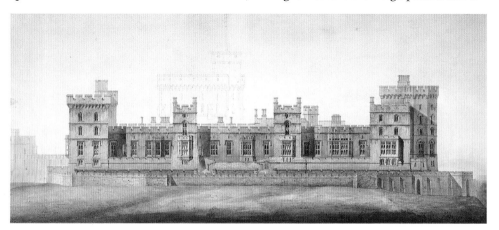

LEFT
Joseph Nash (1709–78), *The East Terrace garden*, 1848 (detail). Lithograph. George IV's work extended to the gardens surrounding the Castle. On the east front, he laid out a D-shaped parterre of beds, bordered by raised walks and punctuated by numerous marble and bronze statues and vases, brought to Windsor from several of the older palaces, including Hampton Court.

gothicise his own surname, which he changed to the more Norman-sounding Wyatville. Inside the Castle, a new suite of rooms facing east was fitted out in the grandest manner, partly incorporating fixtures such as chimneypieces and panelling from Carlton House, the King's former London residence, dismantled after he ascended the throne. The firm of Morel & Seddon was awarded a contract amounting to £270,000 for the interior decoration, including the supply of modern furnishings – seat furniture, bedroom suites and upholstery, much of it in the latest French Empire style. In addition, George IV and Long embarked on a determined campaign to acquire antique furniture, tapestries and bronzes in salerooms and through agents in France.

George IV took up residence in the Castle in 1828. His improvements, eventually costing nearly £300,000, were widely praised. Lady Dover, on seeing the Grand Corridor in 1829, wrote that it was 'the most strikingly beautiful thing you can conceive', while Lady Georgiana Ellis found that the extensive use of gold leaf contributed a 'fairy-like appearance' to the new apartments. The King died just 18 months later, in June 1830, aged 67. The refurbishment continued under Wyatville's direction, but on a reduced budget.

RIGHT
Morel & Seddon, *Design for the Large Drawing Room* (Crimson Drawing Room), *c.*1826. Watercolour.

ABOVE
Sir Edwin Landseer
(1802–73), *Windsor Castle
in Modern Times*, 1840–43.
Throughout the 20 years
of their married life, the
royal couple received at
Windsor the artists and
sculptors who created
their best-known
likenesses, such as the
painters Edwin Landseer
and Franz Xaver
Winterhalter (1805–73),
and the sculptors Carlo
Marochetti (1805–67) and
Joseph Edgar Boehm
(1834–90).

The Castle enjoyed a golden age during the long reign of Queen Victoria (r.1837–1901). It served as both a rural retreat from London and a magnificent palace in which to entertain, while the Home and Great Parks provided a setting for some of Prince Albert's interests. The Prince (1819–61) designed model farms and a dairy, and a vast kitchen garden, capable of providing fresh fruit, vegetables and flowers for the royal family at all times of year. He also reorganised the Royal Library, and created the Print Room at the north-western end of the State Apartments, classifying and reordering its rich holdings, and assembling a remarkable collection of reproductions of the works of Raphael (1483–1520).

Queen Victoria spent the greatest portion of each year at Windsor, which became the setting for family gatherings and entertainments, in addition to state occasions. The weddings of her eldest children were celebrated there. Visiting celebrities, from Franz Liszt to Buffalo Bill, came and performed for the royal family. King Louis-Philippe of France (1793–1850) and Tsar Nicholas I of Russia (1796–1855) were entertained in state at Windsor in 1844, as were the Emperor Napoleon III (1808–73) in 1855 and a succession of other crowned heads and dignitaries. The Castle became the focus for the expanding British Empire and for much of royal Europe, many of whose families were related to the Queen.

Queen Victoria decided that the State Apartments should be opened regularly to the public from the 1840s, and during the second half of the century, around 60,000 visitors passed through the rooms each year. From 1842, Brunel's Great Western Railway brought Windsor within range for a day trip

MUSIC AND PERFORMANCE

Throughout Queen Victoria's reign, the Castle was used for musical and theatrical entertainments. Many composers and soloists played in private for Queen Victoria at Windsor, including Ignacy Paderewski (1860–1941) in 1891, and Franz Liszt (1811–86) and Edvard Grieg (1843–1907) in 1897. Schubert's 'Great' C major symphony was performed by the Queen's private band during a concert in the Waterloo Chamber. Throughout the 1850s, theatrical seasons were held in the King's Drawing Room, with productions of Shakespeare and contemporary plays masterminded by the actor-manager Charles Kean. Such performances have remained a Windsor tradition.

ABOVE

Joseph Nash, *Queen Victoria and Louis-Philippe of France driving out from the Quadrangle, 10 October 1844*, 1844. Watercolour. The charabanc was a gift of the French monarch and survives in the Royal Mews at Buckingham Palace.

from London, and the Queen herself began to use the train for her journeys to and from the capital.

Following George IV's comprehensive restoration, very little needed to be done to the Castle during Queen Victoria's reign, but some essentials remained to be completed. Within the State Apartments, a new private chapel, designed by Edward Blore (1787–1879), was created at the eastern end of St George's Hall, and modern heating and fire precautions were introduced. In 1867, Wyatville's Grand Staircase was replaced by another, rising in a different direction, designed by Anthony Salvin (1799–1881). In 1863, Salvin had rebuilt the Guard Room and the Curfew Tower in the Lower Ward. The adjacent Horseshoe Cloister was rebuilt to the designs of Sir George Gilbert Scott (1811–78) in 1871.

FROGMORE

The Frogmore estate was acquired for the use of Queen Charlotte and her daughters and was added to the Home Park in the 1840s. The seventeenth-century Frogmore House, enlarged by James Wyatt in the 1790s, was the country residence of Queen Victoria's mother, the Duchess of Kent, and is still used regularly by the Royal Family. It is open to the public on certain days in May and August.

Immediately after Prince Albert's death at Windsor in 1861, Queen Victoria employed the architect A.J. Humbert (1822–77) and Ludwig Gruner (1801–82), Prince Albert's chief artistic adviser, to construct the Royal Mausoleum in the grounds of Frogmore House. After the Queen's own death in 1901, she too was buried there. (The Mausoleum is not currently on the visitor route.)

THE TWENTIETH CENTURY

On ascending the throne in 1901, King Edward VII reacted against the rather sombre and increasingly cluttered character that the interior of the Castle had acquired during the latter part of Queen Victoria's reign. The Grand Vestibule and Queen's Guard Chamber, in particular, had filled up with innumerable gifts, brought by state visitors or presented at the time of the Golden and Diamond Jubilees in 1887 and 1897. The new King simplified and rearranged the contents of many of these and other rooms, and modernised the private apartments, extending the use of electric lighting and introducing central heating and bathrooms. The Surveyor of The King's Works of Art, Guy Laking (1875–1919), redisplayed the armour and trophies on the Grand Staircase and in the Guard Chamber and St George's Hall; and the principal State Apartments were rehung with silk damask and the pictures cleaned.

King George V (r.1910–36), the first monarch of the new House of Windsor (the German style of the House of Saxe-Coburg having been dropped in 1917, during the First World War), continued this work with his consort, Queen Mary (1867–1953). In the energy she devoted to the preservation of Windsor and its collections, Queen Mary was driven by a pride in her

family's history and a real understanding of the symbolic importance of the Castle in dangerous times. The First World War had brought two of Queen Victoria's grandchildren, King George V and Kaiser Wilhelm II (1859–1941), into direct conflict.

Following the renewed outbreak of war in Europe in 1939, Queen Mary's daughter-in-law, Queen Elizabeth (1900–2002), consort of King George VI (r.1936–52), commissioned a series of views of Windsor from John Piper (1903–92), inspired by those made in the time of George III by Paul Sandby (1731–1809). The paintings were a contribution to the recording of national monuments in the face of the threat from the air. At the height of the bombardments in 1940, while the King and Queen resolutely remained at Buckingham Palace, the Princesses Elizabeth and Margaret (1930–2002) (then aged 14

and 9) lived at Windsor, where their parents joined them each weekend. Each Christmas, a pantomime was performed in the Waterloo Chamber, where temporary murals were fitted to the frames vacated by Sir Thomas Lawrence's great series of portraits, which had been removed for safety.

RIGHT
John Piper, *The Round Tower from the roof of St George's Chapel*, c.1942–9. Watercolour, gouache, pen and black ink.

THE FIRE OF 1992

The wartime bombing raids left Windsor remarkably unscathed. Fifty years later, on 20 November 1992, a far greater catastrophe came, in the form of the fire that broke out in Queen Victoria's private chapel. It is thought to have been caused by a spotlight igniting a curtain above the altar. The fire spread rapidly through the roof-spaces, destroying the ceilings of St George's Hall and the Grand Reception Room, as well as gutting the private chapel, State Dining Room, Crimson Drawing Room and dozens of ancillary rooms on adjacent floors. After a 15-hour struggle by 200 firefighters from seven brigades, the fire was restricted to the north-eastern corner of the Castle. Despite this, thousands of works of art from the Upper Ward, including much of the

contents of the Library and Print Room, were temporarily evacuated as a precaution. By a stroke of good fortune, the fire only affected areas previously emptied of their contents to allow the renewal of electrical wiring and other services. The survival of

ABOVE RIGHT
The charred roof of the Grand Reception Room after the fire.

RIGHT
The burning Castle, from the north-east.

so many great works of art, which had been acquired or commissioned for the damaged rooms, was an important consideration in the debate about the reconstruction.

Repair and restoration began immediately after the fire. The most urgent tasks were to protect the exposed building from the elements and to dry it out:

BELOW
Re-laying the floor in the Grand Reception Room.

1.5 million gallons of water had been pumped into the ancient masonry and timbers. The Duke of Edinburgh chaired the Restoration Committee, which oversaw the project as a whole, while The Prince of Wales presided over the Art and Design Committee. Generally, those areas that had been most badly damaged – such as St George's Hall – were redesigned in a modern Gothic style, by Giles Downes of the Sidell Gibson partnership; the other areas were restored by Donald Insall Associates to the condition in which they had been left by Wyatville and George IV. The work was completed on 20 November 1997, the Golden Wedding Anniversary of The Queen and The Duke of Edinburgh, and exactly five years after the outbreak of the fire. The cost, £37 million, was largely met from the proceeds of admissions to the Castle precincts and to Buckingham Palace, which was opened to the public for the first time in 1993, supplemented by funds from the existing parliamentary grant for the maintenance of the Castle.

The reconstruction process brought many benefits. Much more is now known about the early history of the Castle as the result of extensive archaeological work by English Heritage, and although the task of maintenance is never-ending, the Castle is now in better condition than at any time for the last 200 years.

Tour of the Castle

CASTLE HILL, THE MIDDLE WARD AND NORTH TERRACE

The modern visitor approaches the Castle along the line of an ancient road towards the east. The area was re-landscaped in 2002 for The Queen's Golden Jubilee.

The visitor moves through the Middle Ward – centred on the Round Tower – towards the North Terrace, along the north side of the Upper Ward. The North Terrace was adapted as part of Charles II's restoration of the Castle in the 1670s. During the eighteenth and early nineteenth centuries, the public were admitted to the terraces around the Castle, and George III and his family would often promenade with them. A band played on the East Terrace most days; on Sundays, the Castle residents and local townsfolk were joined by crowds from the surrounding countryside and London. The North Terrace was extended by Wyatville in the 1820s, along the northern edge of the East Terrace Garden, to provide magnificent views of the east front.

LEFT
Paul Sandby, *View of the 'Elizabethan' gate on Castle Hill, c.1765.* Watercolour.

OPPOSITE
The Moat Garden and the Norman Gate. Since the eighteenth century, the moat surrounding the Round Tower has been maintained as an ornamental garden attached to the residence of the Constable and Governor.

QUEEN MARY'S DOLLS' HOUSE

ABOVE
The Dolls' House garden, with benches and wrought-iron gates also designed by Lutyens. The six cypress trees are made of real twigs from Dartmoor.

electricity, and is filled with thousands of objects made by leading artists, designers and craftsmen, on the tiny scale of 1 to 12. It has been described as 'a monument in minute perfection of all that was best in British workmanship'. The garden was designed by Gertrude Jekyll (1843–1932) and is ingeniously housed in the basement drawer.

The finished house was shown at the British Empire Exhibition at Wembley in 1924, where it was seen by more than 1.5 million people. The following year, it was lent to the Ideal Home Exhibition at Olympia, where an extra charge of a shilling was made to view it, in aid of the Queen's Charitable Fund. A portion of each visitor's entrance fee is still donated to charity.

RIGHT
A wind-up gramophone from the Nursery in Queen Mary's Dolls' House. Just 14cm high, it comes with records such as 'Rule Britannia' and 'God Save the King'.

This famous dolls' house, built for Queen Mary in 1924, was never intended as a child's plaything. It was initiated by King George V's cousin, Princess Marie Louise (1872–1956), and the architect Sir Edwin Lutyens (1869–1944). Lutyens intended to make an accurate record of an aristocratic London house of the time. The house has running water and

DRAWINGS GALLERY

CHINA MUSEUM

This handsome vaulted undercroft was designed by James Wyatt for George III, between 1800 and 1804, to house the new Grand Staircase, an arrangement superseded by Jeffry Wyatville's alterations. The central part of the undercroft, which had formerly housed the stairs, was then vaulted over, and the resulting Gothic hall linked the State Entrance and new Grand Staircase. This arrangement ceased in 1867, when Anthony Salvin realigned the Grand Staircase for Queen Victoria. The space is now used as an exhibition gallery for temporary displays from the Royal Collection.

During the reign of Queen Victoria, this room, known as the Museum, was used to display state gifts. The Ionic stone columns date from Hugh May's remodelling in the 1670s. They were reused here during Salvin's work of the 1860s.

ABOVE
Plate from the Tournai service, *c.*1787.

LEFT
Items from the Worcester dessert service. This richly gilded service, commissioned by William IV in 1830, is still used to ornament the table for the annual luncheon of the Knights and Ladies of the Garter.

GRAND STAIRCASE AND GRAND VESTIBULE

The site of the Grand Staircase was originally an internal courtyard, known as Brick Court. Jeffry Wyatville added the glazed Gothic lantern roof, which survived the realignment of the staircase in the 1860s. The trophies of arms and armour that line the walls are based on an arrangement made for William IV (r.1830–37) in the 1830s. All visitors to the State Apartments, whether members of the public or heads of state, ascend this magnificent staircase to begin their tour. Heads of state and guests of The Queen enter via the State Entrance in the Quadrangle and approach the staircase from its southern side.

The Grand Vestibule has changed dramatically over the past three centuries. In the late seventeenth century, it housed the richly decorated Queen's Great Staircase, which led up to the Queen's apartments. The remarkable plaster, fan-vaulted ceiling and lantern are among the few survivors of James Wyatt's later work for George III. The cipher of William IV was added to the ceiling after the stairs were demolished and the Grand Vestibule was created by Wyatt's nephew, Jeffry Wyatville.

The Gothic canopy and showcases were installed in 1888, the year after Queen Victoria's Golden Jubilee, to display some of the thousands of gifts presented from all corners of the Empire. They now hold an important and disparate group of arms and relics, the majority from the collection of George IV.

35

TREASURES OF THE CASTLE

The exceptional collection of drawings housed in the Print Room of the Royal Library has been assembled over the past 500 years. It includes major works by Holbein (1497/8–1543), Michelangelo (1475–1564), Raphael, Parmigianino (1503–40), Guercino (1591–1666) and Canaletto (1697–1768), among others. The greatest treasure of the Royal Library is the unparalleled collection of 600 drawings by Leonardo da Vinci (1452–1519).

ABOVE
William Walls
(*fl.* 1761–5), door lock, presented to George III in 1765. The lock incorporates two pistols, designed to fire in the event of tampering.

BELOW
Ivory throne and footstool, presented to Queen Victoria in 1851 by the Maharajah of Travancore in southern India and displayed as the centrepiece of the Indian Court at the Great Exhibition. In 1877, when she was proclaimed Empress of India, Queen Victoria was photographed on the throne. It remained under the canopy in the Garter Throne Room until the Queen's death in 1901, and has recently been returned to this position (see page 65).

ABOVE
The musket ball that killed Lord Nelson (1758–1805). Nelson was struck in the left shoulder while on the deck of HMS *Victory* during the Battle of Trafalgar in 1805. The ball was removed by the ship's surgeon shortly after Nelson's death and made into a pendant locket, which was later presented to Queen Victoria.

ABOVE
Pieces from the Rockingham service. Probably the most ambitious porcelain service ever made by a British factory, this service was ordered by William IV in 1830, but not delivered until 1837. The decoration of individual pieces celebrates Britain's maritime achievements and expanding Empire, with scenes of India and the Caribbean, and wonderfully modelled pineapples, sugar cane, exotic fruits, coral and shells. Parts of the service are displayed during state banquets.

ABOVE

In the central case of the Grand Vestibule are relics and arms and armour from the magnificent palace of Tipu, Sultan of Mysore at Seringapatam, in southern India. Known as the Tiger of Mysore, Tipu (1750–99) was a ferocious opponent of the British in India. The life-size tiger's head from Tipu's throne, made of gold with rock crystal teeth, was presented to William IV by the East India Company in 1831.

ABOVE

Hans Holbein the Younger, *Sir John Godsalve*, *c*.1532–4. Chalks, pen and ink, and bodycolour.

ABOVE

Leonardo da Vinci, *Study for St James in the Last Supper*, *c*.1495. Red chalk and pen and ink.

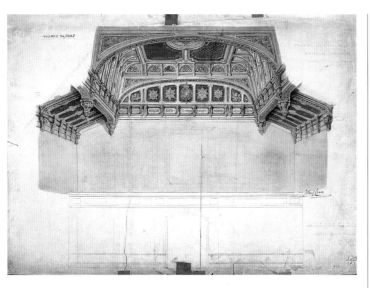

ABOVE
Frederick Crace
(1779–1859), *Design for
the roof of the Waterloo
Chamber*, 1835.
Watercolour.

This vast room was designed by Jeffry Wyatville for George IV, but was completed in the reign of his successor, William IV. It was created to display Sir Thomas Lawrence's portraits, painted to celebrate the success of the forces of Great Britain, Austria, Prussia and Russia at the Battle of Waterloo in June 1815, when Napoleon Bonaparte was finally defeated. The new room filled in an open court that had survived since the thirteenth century. Visitors crossed the open courtyard at ground-floor level and ascended a staircase to the King's Guard Chamber (now the Grand Reception Room). Open colonnades decorated with baroque wall paintings and gilded statues surrounded the courtyard.

The panelled walls of the Waterloo Chamber are applied with limewood carvings, most of which date from the 1680s, carved by Grinling Gibbons and his assistants. They were salvaged from the former Royal Chapel during its demolition in the 1820s. The ingenious roof, decorated by the firm of Crace, has a raking clerestory reminiscent of a ship's timbers. The Indian carpet was woven for this room by the inmates of Agra prison for Queen Victoria's Golden Jubilee, finally reaching Windsor in 1894. Thought to be the largest seamless carpet in existence, it weighs 2 tonnes; during the 1992 fire, it took 50 soldiers to roll it up and move it to safety. The room itself was spared by the thickness of the medieval wall dividing it from St George's Hall.

The Garter Luncheon, given by The Queen for the Knights and Ladies of the Garter, is held here each June. The table is set for 50 to 60 guests, with magnificent gilt dining silver from George IV's Grand Service and the Worcester porcelain service, and the guests are entertained by a band playing on the balcony.

LEFT
Princess Elizabeth
performing in a
pantomime in the
Waterloo Chamber, 1943.

Sir Thomas Lawrence, *Arthur Wellesley, 1st Duke of Wellington*, 1814–15. Sir Thomas Lawrence, Britain's leading portraitist, was chosen by George IV to paint many of the victorious allied monarchs, statesmen and commanders. The eastern wall is dominated by the portrait of the Duke of Wellington (1769–1852), who led the allied forces at Waterloo.

STATE APARTMENTS

The sequence of rooms built for Charles II and his Queen, Catherine of Braganza, between 1675 and 1678, formed the grandest sequence of baroque State Apartments in England, with elaborate painted ceilings and panelled walls, ornamented with superb carvings by Grinling Gibbons and his assistants. The rooms have subsequently been much altered: the panelling was replaced by silk hangings in George III's reign (renewed many times since), and all but three of the original painted ceilings by Antonio Verrio were renewed in ornamental plaster by Francis Bernasconi (1762–1841), under Wyatville's direction. Yet many of the original cornices, dados and carvings can still be seen.

KING'S DRAWING ROOM

This was Charles II's withdrawing room, where he received important visitors and held court assemblies. His grooms-in-waiting slept here. The room marked the divide between the public ante-rooms to the east and the King's private apartments to the west. Courtiers and other 'people of quality' would gather here each morning to pay their respects. The room preserves almost nothing of its seventeenth-century appearance; only the cornice, carved in Grinling Gibbons's workshop, survives.

George IV's body lay in

state here in 1830. The room was draped with black velvet and lit by candlelight. His niece, Queen Victoria, later held regular theatrical performances here – on a stage erected at the north end.

In Queen Victoria's reign, the works of single artists were gathered together in three of the principal State Apartments and the rooms renamed accordingly. Hung entirely with works by (or then thought to be by) the great Flemish baroque painter, Peter Paul Rubens (1577–1640), this room became the Rubens Room. It was redecorated in 2005–6.

PAINTINGS AT WINDSOR

RIGHT
Sir Anthony Van Dyck, *St Martin dividing his cloak*, c.1618 (in the King's Drawing Room).

BELOW RIGHT
John Riley (1646–92), *Bridget Holmes*, 1686. Bridget Holmes was a 'necessary woman', whose responsibilities included the disposal of the contents of chamber pots. She is depicted at the age of 96. She died in her centenary year, having served in four reigns. The painting (in the King's Dining Room) was probably commissioned by James II and is without parallel in its grandeur as a portrait of a servant.

LEFT
Sir Godfrey Kneller, *Michael Alphonsus Shen Fu-Tsung, 'The Chinese Convert'*, 1687 (in the King's Dining Room). Shen Fu-Tsung was one of a party of Chinese who left Macao in 1681 to travel to Europe, at the invitation of the Procurator of the Jesuit Order in Rome. In 1687–8, he helped to catalogue Chinese texts at the Bodleian Library, Oxford.

BELOW LEFT
Agnolo Bronzino (1503–72), *Portrait of a lady in green*, c.1530. From the collection of Charles I (in the King's Closet).

ABOVE
Pieter Bruegel the Elder
(1525–69), *The Massacre
of the Innocents*, 1565–7
(in the King's Dressing
Room).

KING'S BEDCHAMBER

Charles II used this room for the formal ceremonies of *levée* and *couchée*, when, following Louis XIV's example, the King officially rose and went to bed, attended by members of the court; as at Versailles, a low balustrade divided the room – as Celia Fiennes put it in her *Diary* of 1702, 'to secure the bed from the common'. Although he listened to sermons and occasionally dined here, it is thought that Charles II more routinely slept in the small bedchamber next door.

Access to the King's Bedchamber was limited. Here the King met his ministers and other advisers and transacted confidential affairs of state. The present appearance of the room is due partly to George III, who first introduced the crimson silk wall covering, which replaced the seventeenth-century panelling.

KING'S DRESSING ROOM

This small, intimate space was Charles II's Little Bedchamber, where he most probably slept. However, the King was often elsewhere; he installed one of his favourites, Louise de Kéroualle, Duchess of Portsmouth (1649–1734), in a suite immediately below, and another, Nell Gwyn (1650–87), in a large house to the south of the Castle. By 1696, the room was known as the 'king's customary bedchamber'. In the 1830s, Wyatville installed the plaster ceiling with the arms and cipher of William IV, anchors and tridents – motifs that refer to the 'sailor' King's career in the navy before his accession. The room's current name derives from later use as a visiting king's dressing room.

KING'S CLOSET

LEFT
Giovanni Bellini
(c.1431/6–1516), *Portrait of a young man*, c.1507.

The room was created from two smaller rooms for George III in 1804. This was the site of Charles II's Closet – his most private space, to which only the King and his trusted servant, William Chiffinch (c.1602–91), had keys. Here, where the King kept some of his most precious treasures, he could escape from court life.

The plaster ceiling was added for William IV in 1833 and incorporates the arms and cipher of his consort, Adelaide of Saxe-Meiningen (1792–1849). Today, it contains some of the finest Italian Renaissance paintings in the Royal Collection.

LEFT
Rembrandt van Rijn
(1606–69), *Self-portrait in a flat cap*, 1642.

QUEEN'S DRAWING ROOM

This room was designed by Hugh May as Catherine of Braganza's withdrawing room. According to the conventions of the time, it was towards the end of a sequence of apartments designated for her use. Queen Catherine's bedchamber and private apartments originally continued to the west, but were incorporated into the Royal Library in the 1830s.

Like the King's apartments, the Queen's Drawing Room was originally hung with tapestry, and had a ceiling painted with an assembly of the gods. This was replaced, in 1834, with a plaster ceiling loosely based on seventeenth-century designs, incorporating the arms of William IV and Queen Adelaide. During the nineteenth century this room, then called the Picture Gallery, was densely hung with Old Masters.

Today, some of the finest Tudor and Stuart royal portraits in the Royal Collection are hung here.

LEFT
Robert Peake the Elder
(*fl.* 1576–1619), *Henry,
Prince of Wales, in the
hunting field with Robert
Devereux, 3rd Earl of Essex,*
c.1605.

KING'S DINING ROOM

This was Charles II's dining room. The ceiling – one of three by Antonio Verrio that remain from the 1670s – is painted with a banquet of the gods.

The room originally overlooked Brick Court, which was open to the sky until the 1820s. It lies between the King's and the Queen's apartments, so that both the King and the Queen could eat here. The alcoves were intended for the use of servants and musicians; the skylights were added in the 1860s.

RIGHT
Turkey painted by Antonio Verrio in the cove of the ceiling of the King's Dining Room.

LEFT
French Boulle marquetry pedestal clock (detail), late seventeenth century. Purchased by George IV, 1820.

QUEEN'S BALLROOM

Built as a dancing chamber for Catherine of Braganza, this remained the principal ballroom in the Castle until the completion of the Grand Reception Room and Waterloo Chamber in the 1830s. The room was remodelled by Wyatville, who replaced Verrio's ceiling painting, *Charles II giving freedom to Europe*, and removed the oak panelling. The magnificent glass chandeliers were hung during the reign of Queen Victoria. Also at this time, the room was first hung exclusively with portraits by Anthony Van Dyck, an arrangement that continues.

ABOVE
Sir Anthony Van Dyck,
*The five eldest children of
Charles I*, 1637.

SILVER FURNITURE

The late seventeenth-century silver furniture in the Queen's Ballroom is an exceptionally rare survival of a fashion started by Louis XIV at Versailles. The Royal Collection originally had six sets of silver mirrors and tables, together with many wall sconces, chandeliers and sets of fireplace furniture. Such extremely expensive pieces were among the ultimate symbols of prestige and power. Many sets were later melted for the value of their silver.

ABOVE
Among the decorative features of this silver table, made for William III in 1699, is a pineapple, then a great novelty, resting at the centre of the waved stretchers under the table.

QUEEN'S AUDIENCE CHAMBER

This room and the adjoining Queen's Presence Chamber retain their painted ceilings by Verrio, with panelling and carvings by Grinling Gibbons and his assistants, and evoke the original appearance of the King's and Queen's apartments.

Antonio Verrio's ceiling depicts Catherine of Braganza in a chariot, being drawn by swans towards a temple of virtue.

QUEEN'S PRESENCE CHAMBER

The Presence Chamber was the most accessible and public of the Queen's apartments. It was also used as a waiting room for visitors. The painted ceiling depicts Catherine of Braganza seated under a canopy held by zephyrs, while figures of Envy and Sedition retreat before the outstretched Sword of Justice (see page 40).

TAPESTRIES

Tapestries would have been hung in all of the King's and Queen's apartments in Charles II's time. Because they were very costly, they would only be exposed to light when the King and Queen were in residence. The tapestries now displayed here and in the Queen's Presence Chamber were acquired by George IV in the 1820s.

ABOVE
Robert Adam, Marble chimneypiece, 1760s. This was designed for Queen Charlotte's Saloon at Buckingham House. In 1789 the clock was added, with a movement by B.L. Vulliamy and marble figures by John Bacon (1740–99). The chimneypiece was moved from London to Windsor in the 1830s.

QUEEN'S GUARD CHAMBER

From the late seventeenth century, the Queen's Guard Chamber marked the entrance to the Queen's apartments. Visitors ascended the Queen's Stair on the site of the adjoining Grand Vestibule. Here, the Yeomen of the Guard stopped unauthorised people from progressing further.

As it now appears, the Guard Chamber is the work of Wyatville, who enlarged the room by adding the bay to the south. This provides views across the Quadrangle to the George IV Gateway, beyond which the Long Walk stretches south. The decorative displays of arms on the walls are simplified versions of seventeenth-century arrangements of standard-issue weaponry. In the display cases are examples of more ornate arms and armour, many of which came from George IV's collection at Carlton House.

LEFT
Sir Francis Chantrey, *Admiral Lord Nelson*, 1835. The Guard Chamber is dominated by this colossal marble bust, commissioned for this room by William IV and completed in 1835.

ABOVE
Joseph Nash, *The Queen's Guard Chamber*, 1848. Lithograph.

ST GEORGE'S HALL

This magnificent hall (55.5 x 9 metres) was created for George IV by Wyatville, who combined two adjacent spaces, St George's Hall and the Royal Chapel, to form one long apartment. Both rooms had magnificent baroque murals and ceilings by Verrio and carvings by Grinling Gibbons, all of which was dismantled by Wyatville. The painted ceiling was replaced with plain plasterwork, studded with the coats of arms of all the Knights of the Garter since the foundation of the Order in 1348, with grained plaster ribs at intervals.

During the fire of 20 November 1992, the ceiling, roof and east end wall were entirely destroyed and the remainder of the Hall was seriously damaged. When it came to be restored, the decision was taken to replace Wyatville's ceiling with a new hammer-beam roof, designed by Giles Downes of the Sidell Gibson Partnership. Constructed entirely of green oak, using medieval carpentry techniques, it is the largest timber roof built in the twentieth century. The blank shields on the ceiling are the erased arms of those 'degraded' Knights expelled from the Order at different times. The names of all Knights, past and present, are inscribed on the panels around the Hall, together with the date of their installation and the corresponding number of their coat of arms.

THE KING'S CHAMPION

The armoured figure of the King's Champion on horseback dominates the east end of the Hall. The Champion used to ride into the coronation banquet held in Westminster Hall, following the coronation ceremony in the Abbey. The Champion would throw down his gauntlet three times and challenge anyone to deny the authority of the new sovereign. The last such event took place after the coronation of George IV in 1821. The figure shown here wears a suit of armour made for Sir Christopher Hatton (1540–91) in 1585, and subsequently given by him to Robert Dudley, Earl of Leicester (1532–88), favourite of Elizabeth I. It was worn by the King's Champion at the coronations of George I and George II.

The screen at the east end, also a new addition, supports carvings of the Queen's Beasts, given by the Corporation of London in support of the fire restoration and to mark the Golden Wedding Anniversary of The Queen and The Duke of Edinburgh. The huge silvered and painted plaster Garter and rose on the wall behind was presented by the nations of the Commonwealth. The 53 petals represent the member countries. The design was taken from a fifteenth-century lockplate in St George's Chapel.

St George's Hall has had a continuous association with the Order of the Garter for 600 years. In June each year, The Queen, The Duke of Edinburgh and the other 24 Knights assemble here before processing to St George's Chapel for their annual service.

The Hall is also used for state banquets, held at the beginning of a State Visit. The dining table, normally kept in the Waterloo Chamber, is extended to its full length of 47.5 metres and seats 160 people.

LANTERN LOBBY

This room was created after the 1992 fire, on the site of the former private chapel where the fire had broken out. The chapel had been created for Queen Victoria, to a somewhat unsatisfactory design by Edward Blore. During the restoration, it was decided to relocate the chapel and allow a processional route between the State and Semi-State Apartments; the octagonal Lantern Lobby conveniently turns the axis between the two. It was designed by Giles Downes in a modern Gothic style, partly inspired by Ely Cathedral and the Abbey of Batalha in Portugal. The columns, vaults and balustrade are constructed from laminated oak, a modern technique, which contrasts with that used for the roof of St George's Hall. On the floor, the badge and motto of the Garter are inlaid in British marbles. The red stone that forms the cross in the centre was a gift from the Duke of Devonshire; it is from a very small deposit on his estate in Derbyshire and is known as 'The Duke's Red'.

SILVER GILT

The Lantern Lobby was partly conceived as a treasury. In the wall cases are displayed some of the finest examples of gilded silver in the Royal Collection.

ABOVE George Wickes, centrepiece, 1745.

RIGHT
Sir Gerald Kelly,
*Queen Elizabeth, Consort
of King George VI*, 1942–5.
This portrait and that of
King George VI (far right)
are on display in the
Crimson Drawing Room.

FAR RIGHT
Sir Gerald Kelly,
King George VI, 1942–5.

This glittering sequence of rooms was created for George IV in the 1820s. Originally built as the King's private apartments, they are now used by The Queen for entertaining and are open to the public only during the winter months.

Following his accession in 1820, George IV decided not to live in the north range, the site of the King's apartments since the twelfth century, preferring the eastern and southern ranges where his mother and sisters had lived. This group of apartments was designed by Wyatville as a sequence of drawing rooms, dining rooms and library for the King's private use, and they reflect perfectly George IV's lavish taste.

The interiors were furnished and decorated by Morel & Seddon. The rooms form a superb and unrivalled sequence, widely regarded as the finest and most complete expression of later Georgian taste in Britain.

The Semi-State Apartments were severely damaged by the 1992 fire. In preparation for a rewiring project, they had previously been cleared of most of their contents, an important factor in the decision to restore the rooms to their original condition. The finishes had become subdued during the intervening 170 years and the restoration project enabled a return to their intended sparkling magnificence.

GREEN DRAWING ROOM

This was originally planned as a library, flanked by the White Drawing Room to the south (not open to the public) and the Crimson Drawing Room to the north. All three rooms conform to George IV's favourite plan of a long room with a large bay window in the centre at one side. The ceiling is perhaps Wyatville's most accomplished at Windsor.

Although the fire only damaged the northern end of the room, the rest was soaked with water. The magnificent carpet, which survived the fire, is now considered too delicate to allow visitors to walk on it. It was specifically designed for this room by Ludwig Gruner, for Queen Victoria and Prince Albert, and was shown at the Great Exhibition of 1851.

CRIMSON DRAWING ROOM

The principal room in the Semi-State Apartments, the Crimson Drawing Room was severely damaged in the 1992 fire, when the ceiling collapsed and the walls were badly burnt. The steel roof structure expanded in the intense heat and pushed out the eastern wall overlooking the garden, threatening the entire façade with collapse. The restored ceiling incorporates many salvaged fragments of the original.

George IV's decorative scheme was reinstated using Morel & Seddon's original coloured designs, surviving in the Royal Library (see page 23). The black marble chimneypiece, incorporating bronze figures of satyrs, was originally supplied by B.L. Vulliamy for Carlton House in 1807. It survived the fire unscathed, but the splendid chandelier was less fortunate; most of its glass had to be renewed. The parquet floor, designed by Ludwig Gruner in 1854, was damaged beyond repair in the fire and has been replaced. The walls are hung with portraits of George IV's siblings, and the State Portraits of King George VI and Queen Elizabeth by Sir Gerald Kelly (1879–1972), painted at Windsor during the Second World War. Their fictive backgrounds were based on designs by Sir Edwin Lutyens.

ABOVE
The doors in the Crimson Drawing Room incorporate superb carved and gilded limewood trophies from Carlton House, carved by Edward Wyatt between 1811 and 1816. Those at the north end had to be recarved, and the others required extensive restoration.

ABOVE
The magnificent curtains, with their complex fringing and tassels (passementerie), in this and the adjoining rooms, are closely based on Morel & Seddon's designs. Each tassel, of silk thread around a carved boxwood core, was made by hand during the 1990s.

STATE DINING ROOM

Intended as George IV's private dining room, the State Dining Room has since been used for more official entertaining. Queen Victoria, a great believer in fresh air, insisted that all the windows should be thrown open and that the fires should remain unlit during meals, even in winter. Today, Her Majesty The Queen entertains guests here for lunch during Ascot week, and in the evening for 'dine and sleep' parties every Easter.

The Dining Room has twice been damaged by fire, in 1853 and 1992. The later fire completely consumed all the walls, floor and ceiling, and not one decorative element remained. The room has been restored to Wyatville's Gothic design.

ABOVE
Massive Russian porcelain vase, presented to Queen Victoria by Tsar Nicholas I, 1844.

OCTAGON DINING ROOM

This small dining room is used by members of The Queen's Household when the Court is in residence. It occupies the Brunswick Tower, which was built by Wyatville at the north-east corner of the Castle for picturesque effect. During the 1992 fire, the internal floors collapsed and the tower acted as a flue through which flames shot 15 metres into the sky. Miraculously, the marble chimneypiece survived the intense heat. Analysis of the vitrified bricks showed that temperatures had approached 820 degrees Celsius.

CHINA CORRIDOR

This circulation corridor was added by Wyatville outside the medieval curtain wall. The glass cases were originally intended for some of George IV's collection of arms and armour. The displays of porcelain, introduced by Queen Mary in the 1920s, include a large quantity of Chinese and Japanese porcelain of the seventeenth and early eighteenth centuries, and parts of several English and continental dining services.

At the opposite end of the corridor are two English Minton services inspired by French eighteenth-century Sèvres wares. The earlier service, purchased by Queen Victoria from the Great Exhibition in 1851, includes the large 'Victoria' centrepiece, decorated with figures of the four seasons. The second service was made, in 1863, for King Edward VII and Queen Alexandra (1844–1925) when Prince and Princess of Wales.

THE MANCHESTER SERVICE

Made at the Sèvres factory between 1769 and 1783, this dinner and dessert service was an official present from Louis XVI to the Duchess of Manchester (1741–1832), whose husband was appointed ambassador at the court of Versailles in 1783 and concluded the peace negotiations that year, which brought to an end the American War of Independence. George IV purchased the service from the Duchess in 1802.

ABOVE

Pierre-François Cozette (1714–1801) and Audran, *Jason pledges his faith to Medea*, 1776–9. This is one of a set of six Gobelins tapestries, after paintings by Jean-François de Troy.

seventeenth century when the room became the King's Guard Chamber. From here it was possible to enter the King's apartments to the north-west and St George's Hall and the chapel to the south. During the 1992 fire, Bernasconi's plaster ceiling collapsed and the walls were badly burnt and water-damaged. The three chandeliers, just reinstalled following complete restoration and rewiring, were severely damaged, but were once again restored and reinstated. The room itself was entirely restored and all the gilding renewed. The original parquet floor survived the fire; blocks that were singed by the flames have been reversed.

Of all the rooms created for George IV, the Grand Reception Room perhaps best epitomises his love of all things French. Intended as the principal ballroom of the Castle, it is one of the earliest rococo revival interiors in England, starting a fashion that was to last throughout the nineteenth century. The walls incorporate eighteenth-century French panelling, extended in height by the addition of moulded stucco by Francis Bernasconi.

This was the site of Edward III's Great Staircase, at the heart of the medieval palace. The floor still incorporates fourteenth-century roof timbers, reused during the

MALACHITE URN

Presented to Queen Victoria by Tsar Nicholas I in 1839, this is one of the largest examples outside Russia. During the 1992 fire, it filled up with hose water, causing the malachite veneers to fall off in many places and require a lengthy restoration.

GARTER THRONE ROOM

In this room new Knights and Ladies of the Garter are invested with the insignia of the Order by The Queen. It was Queen Victoria's principal Throne Room, where she received important visitors, seated on a magnificent Indian ivory throne (see page 36).

Wyatville created the space by combining the former King's Presence Chamber with the eastern end of the King's Privy or Audience Chamber. The former division between the two rooms is marked by the shallow arch two-thirds of the way in. These two rooms originally lay at the beginning of the King's apartments. The seventeenth-century ceilings were replaced by Wyatville's ingenious design in plaster, incorporating the insignia and collar of the Order of the Garter. The wainscot dado and cornice survive from the seventeenth century, but the oak wall panels were installed by Queen Mary in the 1920s. The limewood carvings by Grinling Gibbons and his assistants were reused from other rooms.

LEFT
Sir Herbert James Gunn (1893–1964), *Queen Elizabeth II*, 1954–6. This is the official or State Portrait of Her Majesty The Queen. She wears her Coronation dress and robe of state, the George and Collar of the Garter, and George IV's Diamond Diadem. She touches the sceptre, and the Imperial State Crown rests on a table beside her.

RIGHT
R.T. Landells (1833–77), *Reception of the Ambassadors of Siam, November 1857*, 1858. Watercolour.

SEMI-STATE APARTMENTS

The Order of the Garter is one of the oldest and most important orders of chivalry in the world. Founded by Edward III in 1348, following his victorious return from France after the Battle of Crécy (1346) and the capture of Calais (1347), it consisted of the Sovereign, the Prince of Wales and 24 Knights Companion, many of whom had fought with the King in France. It is thought that the emblem of the new Order developed from a

strap or band worn in battle. The motto, *Honi soit qui mal y pense* ('Shame on he who thinks evil of it'), has been interpreted as relating to Edward III's claim to the throne of France. An alternative explanation suggests that he uttered these words as he picked up a garter belonging to one of the ladies of the court, and wore it on his person.

A three-day festival for the new Order was observed regularly at Windsor for 200 years. Charles I placed new emphasis on the Order, adding the star badge to the insignia and reviving the annual procession at Windsor on the eve of St George's Day; but after 1674, few festivals were celebrated in their entirety.

On 23 April 1948, King George VI ordered the Knights of the Garter to assemble at Windsor to celebrate the 600th anniversary of the foundation of the Order, and this set the pattern for the annual 'Solemnity of St George' in mid-June, including the service and procession on Garter Day.

Today, the Order consists of distinguished figures in the life of the nation and Commonwealth, including former prime ministers. The Garter is the highest order of chivalry and remains in the gift of the Sovereign.

The military origins of the Order are embodied in the Military Knights of Windsor, retired members of the armed services who live within the Lower Ward and represent the Garter Knights at services in the chapel.

On the foundation of the Order, 26 'poor knights' were appointed to pray for the Sovereign and the Knights of the Order.

The insignia, consisting of the Garter itself, the badge with St George and the dragon, and the eight-pointed star with the cross of St George, can be found throughout the Castle as ornamental motifs.

LOWER WARD

The Lower Ward encompasses the ecclesiastical and collegiate life of St George's Chapel and the residences of the Military Knights of Windsor.

The Guard Room, with its parade ground, is also located here, in a range of buildings against the thirteenth-century west wall.

ABOVE
Memorial by Matthew
Wyatt to King George IV's
daughter, Princess
Charlotte, who died in
childbirth in 1817.

St George's Chapel lies on the north side of the Lower Ward. Work on the present chapel began under Edward IV in 1475; the east end, or Quire (choir), was completed by 1484. The magnificent stone fan vaulting seen by visitors today was added shortly afterwards, by Henry VII. The chapel was finally completed under Henry VIII in 1528, with the fan vault over the crossing.

The spiritual home of the Order of the Garter and the site of a number of royal tombs and memorials, the chapel also ranks as one of the finest examples of the Perpendicular style in the country. This style is characterised by large windows, tall, slender pillars, and an overall impression of soaring grace and elegance. One of the features of note in the nave is the West Window, 11 metres high, and incorporating early sixteenth-century stained glass. Royal memorials in the nave include those of King George V and Queen Mary, and the spectacular monument to George IV's only child, Princess Charlotte (1796–1817), who died in childbirth. King George VI, Queen Elizabeth (The Queen Mother) and Princess Margaret are interred in a memorial chapel off the north Quire aisle. Further tombs and memorials include those of Edward IV, Henry VI, and King Edward VII and Queen Alexandra. The sealed entrance to the vault containing the coffins of Henry VIII and Charles I is under the centre of the Quire.

Visitors can also see some remarkable examples of medieval woodwork and ironwork. The west door of the original chapel (now the Albert Memorial Chapel), dating back to 1240, is preserved in the Ambulatory. The magnificent Sovereign's Stall, used by The Queen today, was constructed in the late eighteenth century.

Treasures of the chapel include Edward III's long sword (2 metres), probably the weapon he wielded in battle. This is in the south, or 'pilgrimage', aisle of the chapel, where visitors can see an alms box, made around 1480 by John Tresilian, to encourage pilgrims to the chapel to leave donations. As well as the tomb of Henry VI – renowned for his piety – pilgrims also came to see the Cross Gneth, a reliquary presented by Edward III and said to have included a portion of the True Cross.

At least three services take place in the chapel every day, and visitors are welcome to attend.

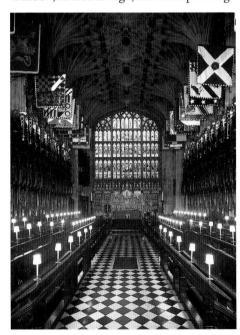

RIGHT
The Quire of St George's
Chapel, looking towards
the altar.

OPPOSITE
The fan-vaulted ceiling
of the Quire, with the
banners of the Knights
of the Garter, 1989.

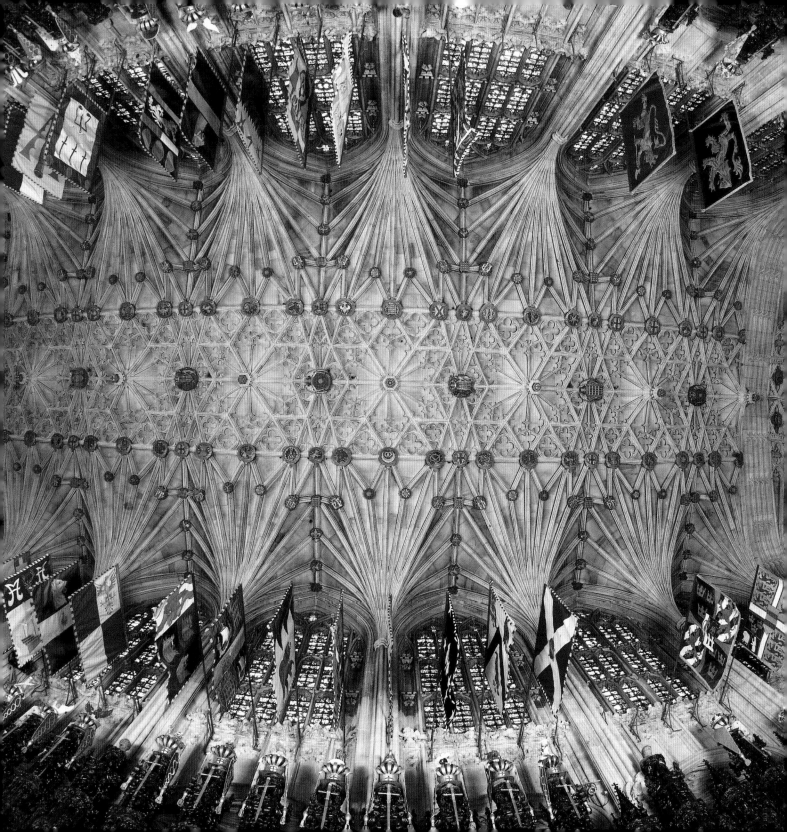

ALBERT MEMORIAL CHAPEL

The richly decorated interior of this chapel, originally built as Henry III's chapel in the 1240s and substantially altered by Henry VII, was created by Sir George Gilbert Scott for Queen Victoria, to commemorate her husband, Prince Albert. The chapel is now dominated by the masterpiece of the sculptor and jeweller Alfred Gilbert (1854–1934), the tomb of the Duke of Clarence and Avondale, King Edward VII's eldest son, who died in 1892.

The Great Park is a large, enclosed area of parkland to the south of Windsor, amounting to just over 2,000 hectares. The origins of the Park pre-date the Norman Conquest. It was created for the protection of the vert (greenery) and venison (chiefly deer) involved in the royal sport of hunting.

In the 1680s, during the reign of Charles II, work began on the planting of a great avenue of 4 kilometres, the Long Walk, which provided a link between the Castle and the Great Park for the first time. The original rows of elm trees eventually died out; they were replaced, in 1945, by the present rows of London plane trees and horse chestnuts.

Surrounding the Castle, to the east, north and south, is the Home Park, a more private area of parkland. The Frogmore estate was added to the Home Park as part of a series of changes in the 1840s and 1850s.

The office of Ranger of the Great Park, with overall responsibility for the Park and its Keepers, was established in the seventeenth century, and since 1746 has been held by members of the royal family. The first Ranger, from 1746 to 1765, was William Augustus, Duke of Cumberland (1721–65), second son of George II. His rangership saw the creation of Virginia Water, a large, ornamental lake at the southern end of the Park, with cascade, grotto and Chinese tea house.

George III, who was keenly interested in agriculture and botany, oversaw the transformation of some areas of the Park for farming purposes. The Park was once again the subject of sustained agricultural improvement during the rangership of Prince Albert. Today, the arable land within the Great Park covers an area of about 485 hectares. Part of the Park is stocked with a herd of red deer, which can often be seen from the Long Walk. The present Ranger is The Duke of Edinburgh, who runs the Great Park with a Deputy Ranger, the Crown Estate Commissioners and staff.

LEFT
Attributed to William Daniell (1769–1837), *Windsor Castle from the Long Walk*, *c*.1825.

71

THE PARKS

BELOW
An oak tree planted *c*.1120, between the Long Walk and Queen Anne's Ride in Windsor Great Park.

OVERLEAF
A procession of carriages approaching the Castle up the Long Walk during the State Visit to Windsor Castle by the President of India, Smt. Pratibha Devisingh Patil, October 2009.